BUT GOD

DR. RITA NEWELL

BUT GOD

Published by Krystal Lee Enterprises (KLE Publishing) Copyright © 2026 by Dr. Rita Newell All rights reserved. Please send comments and questions:

Publisher:
Krystal Lee Enterprises
770-240-0089 Ext. 1
sales@KLEPub.com

To Reach the Author:
Email: lordandelegance@yahoo.com
Phone: (630) 777-8176
Web: www.LordandEleganceMinistries.com
Social Handle: Dr. Rita Newell on Facebook

Printed in the United States of America.

ISBN: **979-8-89987-923-4**

My sister Rita accepted Christ as her Lord and Savior at a very young age, around 12 years old. From that time until now, her faith has been unwavering. She lives by scripture, is a prayer warrior and nurtures others in faith. Her personal relationship with God is constant in her life daily. Whenever she needs an answer to a situation or a problem, she always through prayer and supplication hears God (Proverbs 3:5-6). I love and I'm thankful for my sister Rita. She will leave a spiritual legacy to all that know and love her.

CHARLOTTE NEWELL-MCDUFFIE

At a very young age, it was apparent to anyone who knew Rita Newell that she loved and worshiped God! As she grew into her adulthood, she displayed this in every aspect of her life. No matter if she was at work, attending a family gathering, socializing with friends or in the midst of other believers, testifying, prophesying, and worshiping God. She stands out as a woman of great faith! Her faith, belief, and love of God have not only helped her through trials and tribulations in her life, but the word of God that she is willing to share at any given time, any given setting, also helped those who need to be reminded or even just shown for the first time what a mighty God we serve! Her faith and love of God is magnetic, and anyone in her presence will feel it. She is a true warrior for God and anyone who has the privilege of knowing her will be blessed!

COUSIN BETTY NEWELL-MACEO

Dr. Rita Newell is the kind of woman of God who carries both power and peace. She's deeply rooted in the Word, but just as deeply rooted in love. She listens with her heart, speaks with wisdom, and moves in a way that draws people closer to God without ever needing a spotlight. Her life is a safe place for rest, restoration, and truth, and she doesn't just pray for you, she covers you. She's discerning, bold, nurturing and absolutely allergic to the devil's nonsense. You know when you've been in her presence because something in you shifts for the better.

DR. CARLA STEWART
CLS Comprehensive Services

Dr. Rita Newell is a true builder of the Kingdom of God. She is a faithfully gifted and generous servant, mantled to skillfully wear many hats. You will find Dr. Rita to be a cutting-edge teacher with revelation and insight from heaven. Her strong prophetic grace makes her sensitive to hear what the Spirit is saying to His people and it releases power that brings deliverance to those held captive by the devil. Many have been encouraged and transformed by the wisdom she freely shares. Her years of sacrificial giving, serving and loving will continue to yield a fruitful harvest, all to the glory of the Lord Jesus Christ.
Sincerely submitted,

PROPHET MELODY MORROW CALHOUN

Dr. Rita has been such a blessing to me and my family, pouring into us in ways that have truly made a difference. From the very beginning, she spoke life, encouragement, and wisdom over me with a generosity that felt both genuine and deeply needed. She is so intentional with every word she speaks, making sure it's heard and understood. Even though we haven't known each other long, she has taken me in as her own family – and I've done the same with her. What's being built between us is something that's been prayed over, submitted to the Lord, and cherished more than I can express. Dr. Rita is real, steady, and safe. Our friendship is full of the kind of care and connection that stays with you.

SISTER KIMBERLY EMERY

I met Dr. Rita through my sister who was friends with her niece. She and my sister became really good friends and the result of that was the rest of my family and I were blessed with her friendship as well. I have found her to be one of the most kind, giving, loving and selfless persons I have ever met. Through her, I have learned what real salvation looks like. She has been a pillar for not only me, but my entire family through many storms. She has kept us covered in prayer, was always there to give an encouraging word, never beat us down but was always honest. She always wants God's best for you in every area of your life. Even when she sees you in your worst state, she still encourages you, loves you and reminds you who God says you are. The love of God is always felt in her words, her deeds and the way she sets an example of what Godly living looks like. I feel truly blessed to have this example to learn from.

ALICE BALL

Dr. Rita is one who truly loves God and His people. She lives a life rooted in obedience to God. This is displayed in her life on a daily basis. I have watched her yield in obedience to God, even when it was difficult. I have watched her love beyond an individual's faults. She never sits in judgment on people, but she will tell you the truth in love. I am so grateful that God allowed our paths to cross. I appreciate her for being an amazing example of a woman of God in my life.

RITA D. BALL

PREFACE

      To God be the glory for all the things He has done for me. Without the help of the Holy Spirit, this book could never have been written. I'm blessed to be alive to tell of the demonstrated power of God in my life. As you go on my life's journey while reading this book, my prayer is that God's love, truth, and revelation of who HE is will become more of a reality to you. May God's blessings make you rich in all areas of your life, spiritually, physically, and financially.

Table of Contents

IN THE BEGINNING

Born to the union of Mr. Oscar James and Mrs. Jessie Lee Newell, I was the ninth of ten children. The first two boys died at childbirth. Along with my parents, there were five girls and three boys growing up in our home. From oldest to youngest, my siblings are Gemilla, Dan (deceased), James, Esaw (deceased), Tarrie, Charlotte, myself and Rosie. We came from very humble beginnings. My dad worked construction, and my mother was the Proverbs 31 woman which says:

10 Who can find a virtuous woman? for her price is far above rubies. 11 The heart of her husband doth safely trust in her, so that he shall have no need of spoil. 12 She will do him good and not evil all the days of her life. 13 She seeketh wool, and flax, and worketh willingly with her hands. 14 She is like the merchants' ships; she bringeth her food from afar.

15 She riseth also while it is yet night, and giveth meat to her household. . . 16 She considereth a field, and buyeth it: with the fruit of her hands she planteth a vineyard. 17 She girdeth her loins with strength, and strengtheneth her arms. 18 She perceiveth that her merchandise is good: her candle goeth not

9

out by night. 19 She layeth her hands to the spindle, and her hands hold the distaff.

20 She stretcheth out her hand to the poor; yea, she reacheth forth her hands to the needy. 21 She is not afraid of the snow for her household: for all her household are clothed. 22 She maketh herself coverings of tapestry; her clothing is silk and purple.

25 Strength and honour are her clothing; and she shall rejoice in time to come. 26 She openeth her mouth with wisdom; and in her tongue is the law of kindness. 27 She looketh well to the ways of her household, and eateth not the bread of idleness. 28 Her children arise up, and call her blessed; her husband also, and he praiseth her. 29 Many daughters have done virtuously, but thou excellest them all.

30 Favour is deceitful, and beauty is vain: but a woman that feareth the Lord, she shall be praised. 31 Give her of the fruit of her hands; and let her own works praise her in the gates.

My mother exemplified the above verses in many ways. She was a homemaker who loved God and trusted Him to take care of us. She would wash our clothes with the old-fashioned washing machine. She would push the washed clothes through the wringer and then put them in a plastic basket and take them outside in the backyard to hang on the clothesline to dry. After the clothes dried, she would bring them into the house, pull out the ironing board, and iron our clothes for hours at a time. I would sit and watch her, and I saw how meticulous she was with each item of clothing.

She would cook while we were at school, and when we came home from school for lunch, she had our lunch prepared and ready to eat. After school, we would take off our school clothes, put on play clothes, do our homework, and have dinner. When spring came, she would plant a garden in the back yard, and when the harvest was ripe, she'd pick the vegetables and cook them for dinner. She would rise up early every morning to ensure my dad had break-fast before he left for work, and she'd feed us after we were bathed and dressed for school. Her wisdom was past her level of education. She had the capacity to love all her children and did so gracefully.

Growing up, my father was the provider of the family. He would go to work, come home, change his clothes, eat dinner, watch TV, and go to bed. He was someone in the home with us, but there was not much interaction with him until we became teenag-ers. Our mother was the disciplinarian in the home. She said what she meant and meant what she said. If we lied to her to get out of trouble, that would get us into trouble. Telling her a lie was a true indication of a butt whooping, as she called it.

As a child, while my siblings were outside play-ing, many times I would sit in the house with my mother. I learned compassion and giving firsthand by watching how my mother treated people who were less fortunate than we were. When I was six years old, my friend Ann lived down the block. I was outside in front of the house jumping rope, and Ann came down and said she was hungry. I took her inside and informed my mother that Ann was hungry. My mother fed her breakfast, bathed her, and washed and combed her hair. She sent her home with clothes and food. My mother would give her last if it would help someone in need.

Many times, as a small child, my dad or brothers would come home intoxicated and would put eggs in water and turn the stove on. They would fall asleep at the kitchen table, and the Holy Spirit would wake me up, and the house would be filled with smoke. I would crawl from our bedroom to my parents' bedroom and wake up my mother. She would ask what's burning, and because of the smoke, I couldn't answer her. That happened several times during my childhood, but God took what could have been a tragedy and gave us His mercy. He's a merciful God.

Some of my siblings were very mean to me growing up. I was abused physically by the hands of one of my sisters based on lies her daughter told her. I had a brother who would beat me. Another brother burned my tongue with a 9-volt battery. When I was 19 years old, I got home from work, and one of my siblings hit me. She hit me one time too many, and I lost it. That hit took me to a place that I never want to revisit. Thank God one of my other sisters and brothers were there to intervene, or things would have really gotten out of hand.

Growing up, holidays were huge at our house, especially Thanksgiving and Christmas. My mother would start cooking a week prior and would store the food in the refrigerator located in the basement. She would cook everything you could think of, plus many cakes and pies, all from scratch. As far as I was concerned, she was the best cook in the United States of America. She would tell everyone that dinner would be ready at 1:00 p.m., and it was. We lived in a three-bedroom, one-bathroom bungalow on the south side of Chicago. The family would eat at 1:00 p.m., and guests would start coming around 2:00 p.m. People would be standing in the living room, kitchen, hallway, wherever there was room to get a plate of Momma Jessie's food, and she loved it. My dad would sit at the table in the kitchen and shake his head.

When my siblings got married and had children, I would help take care of my nieces and nephews. Many times, I would get up for their 2:00 a.m. feedings to give my sisters a break. When my siblings' marriages failed, and they needed to come back home to get themselves together, my mother always opened her doors to them and their children. She was the true meaning of a servant. When the kids got a little older, I took them with me to the church I attended, and they remained in church until they became teenagers. I would take them to Sunday School, and they would sing in the youth choir and participate in youth events. I protected them and shielded them from things they didn't need to be part of. They enjoyed coming to church, and things went well for a while.

GROWING UP IN CHURCH

My dad would drop me, my mother, and my youngest sister off at Mt. Calvary Baptist Church in Robbins, Illinois, every Sunday morning. My mother was in the senior choir and served on the usher board. By the time I was six years old, I would tell my mother that the church was boring. When my youngest sister started first grade, my mother began working at Little Company of Mary Hospital. She started sending my sister and I around the corner to what was called the Sanctified Church, and I felt right at home. I accepted the Lord Jesus Christ as my personal savior at an early age, and was the only child saved in my family apart from my mother for many, many years.

On Sunday mornings, I would be the first one up, and my mother would be in the kitchen cooking breakfast for the family. She would have Jubilee Showcase on, and she and I would have our time together before I went to church. I grew up watching The Caravans, Dorothy Love Coates, The Mighty Clouds of Joy, and The Williams Brothers, just to name a few.

To escape sibling rivalry, I would go to church every time the doors were open. I became a member of the Sanctified Church as a child and was an active member for many years. The Pastor had five children, and they were all gifted. The oldest daughter

15

was the organist and Minister of Music, the second oldest daughter was the Directress of the Choir, the oldest son was an organist, the youngest daughter was a pianist, and the youngest son was a drummer. The pastor, his wife, and all his children were singers.

I looked forward to church each week because it was always good singing, preaching, and praising God. I accepted the Lord Jesus Christ as my personal savior as a child. I participated in many auxiliaries of that church from the time I was a child throughout my years as an adult. I held just about every position a person could hold and helped out in any area when I was asked to do so.

When I became a teenager, I began suffering from muscle spasms. One Sunday after church, we traveled to a guest church that afternoon where my Pastor had to preach. We were broadcasting live every Sunday night at that time, and people would tune in from all over the world. We left that service and came back to our church for our Sunday night broadcast. I was sitting in front of the Pastor's wife, and my neck was hurting.

She leaned forward and asked me what was wrong. I told her, and she asked me to bring her the blessed oil. I did, and she put some on my neck and prayed silently. She asked me, "What do you want the radio choir to sing?" One of my favorite songs was "Jesus Can Work It Out," so that's what I told her. I thought it was odd because she had never done that before, but God had a plan.

I was a directress for our Youth Choir at the time, so we sang first, and then the Radio Choir sang. The last song the Radio Choir sang was the one I requested. They ended the song with "Oh Yes!" When they finished that note, the power of God hit me, and I began praising God. I ended up on the other side of the church speaking in tongues. God filled me with His Holy Spirit while praising Him. That experience marked the beginning of many experiences with God.

For many years, I attended church every time the doors were opened. As time went by, members began leaving the church for one reason or another. I hadn't learned that not everyone who professes salvation lives it. I hadn't learned that people are not perfect, so when ugly things began to transpire, I was devastated. I witnessed arguments between the pastor and some of the members. I witnessed men fighting in the church. I witnessed things said in the pulpit that should not have been said. The reason for the church's existence seemed to have gotten buried amidst all the fussing and fighting. When God is no longer the head of a ministry, all forces of hell can prevail against it.

GOD NEVER CHANGES, PEOPLE DO

My Pastor was the President of the State Sunday School Department for many years. All the COGIC churches in the jurisdiction that we were part of came together each year for the Sunday School Convention. It was always a glorious time in the Lord. After some years, my Pastor became a candidate for the position of Bishop of the jurisdiction. He was up against one other person, and the other person won. After my pastor was defeated, I began to witness things that were not in line with God's word.

I realize that when bitterness and unforgiveness sets in, things can become very hostile. It began with the pastor badgering the members for God knows what, and it got worse. Eventually, there was a church split, and I left and went to a different COGIC church along with many of the members, thinking it would be better than where I was. It was like jumping out of the frying pan into a skillet, so I ended up back at the COGIC church I grew up in. Things calmed down for a while.

One Sunday, while we were in Sunday School, the pastor got up to give his review of the Sunday school lesson. Instead of doing so, he began ranting and said something so vulgar that I stood up and told my nieces and nephews to get up and come with me. He yelled at me and told me to sit down. I got my nieces and nephews and left the church. I took them to McDonald's, fed them, and took them to my parents' home. My mother asked why we were home from church so early, and when I shared what happened, she understood why they would not attend anymore. My story is a little different.

GOD ORDERS MY STEPS

I met a young lady named Yvonne Oby (aka Oby) while working at a law firm in 1994. I noticed her because I could see the light of Christ on her countenance. We began eating lunch together in the lunchroom. On Thursdays, when I went into the lunchroom, she would never be there. I asked her one day where she would be on Thursdays, and she told me she taught a Bible Class on her lunch hour at Quaker Oats Company. One day, I asked her if I could accompany her, and she said yes. We became friends, and I began inviting some of my friends to her Bible Class.

Shortly before I met Oby, I bought a brand-new Hyundai Sonata and started having issues with it right off the bat. My dad would drop me off at the train station so I could go to work, and he would take my car into the dealership. After the third time, my dad told them that if he had to bring my car in one more time, they would have to give me a new car, and they agreed. My dream car at the time was the Volvo 940, so one Saturday, I went to Ed Napleton Volvo in Oak Lawn, Illinois. There was a manager named Mr. Steel that I communicated with. I was at the dealership all day, so Mr. Steel asked for my keys to the Sonata and gave me the keys to the black Volvo 940 and said that I could keep it for the weekend. He said, come back Monday, and we'll seal the deal.

Monday, I took a half-day off work so I could go take care of the car business. When I got on the train, the Holy Spirit said, "The dealership sold your car, so the ball is in your court." I was super excited. I got off the train, got in the Volvo, and drove to Ed Napleton Volvo to make the deal. When I got to the dealership, a Christian salesman whom I met on Saturday told me that they sold my Sonata. I smiled at him and was taken to the business manager's office.

The list price of the Volvo was $48,000. The business manager printed out the contract and asked me to sign it. When I look at it, it showed that my car note would be $798 per month. I said, "I'm not paying a $798 dollar car note." Please ask Mr. Steel to come in. The business manager left the office, and when he came back, he didn't say anything. He sat back down at his desk, printed out the contract again, and set it in front of me.

This time, it showed my car note would be $698 per month. I repeated what I said prior and asked for Mr. Steel again. He stormed out of the office, and I'm thinking, what's wrong with this guy? The next time he came in the office, he said nothing, printed out the contract, and slammed it down on the desk in front of me.

I said, "Let me make this clear. I'm not paying $800, $700, $600, or $500 per month for this car. The only thing I will pay will be $400 per month. Now, go get my keys to my Sonata so I can get out of here because I'm not going to keep playing these games with you, and you had better not slam anything else down in front of me." He walked out of the office like he had some sense that time.

The business manager came back into the office after printing out the contract, and it said $398 would be my car note. The Holy Spirit said, ask him how much it would be to install a cut-off switch. I did, and when he told me, I asked him to add it in. The Holy Spirit said, "Now ask him how much the gold package would be." I did and asked him to add it in. It brought my car note to $424 per month. When I saw the final price of the Volvo, the list price was $19,999. Glory to God! They had to come down $30,000 in order for me to have the car note I wanted. God is able to do exceedingly abundantly above all that we ask or think, according to the power that works in us (Ephesians 3:20).

Oby would have Prayer Sessions each year, and I would attend. One year, her main speaker was Bishop Jesse T. Stacks of Detroit, Michigan. He was a prolific scholar of God's word, a doctrinal teacher, and one of God's Prophets. I held on to every word he spoke, bought the tape, and listened to the preached word day in and day out. I heard the Gospel of Jesus Christ for the first time in a way that I never had before. Oby invited Bishop Stacks many times to come and speak at her Prayer Sessions.

During those times, I got to know Bishop Stacks, and he would call me daughter. He would say, "You really should get to know my wife, [Mother Gertrude Stacks]." I remembered Mother Stacks from one of Oby's Prayer Sessions, and she knocked me out the seat and said, "You must pray." I remember laying on the floor saying, "God, who is this lady, and why did she hit me like that?" My friend said it was a shot, so I just looked at her like she was crazy. I told Bishop Stacks, "That's okay, I'm good." He'd just laugh at me and tell me how nice she was.

As time went on, Oby invited me to the "Fellowship Meetings" held every fourth weekend in Detroit, Michigan at Shalom (Bishop Stacks' church). She would speak about Mother Estella Boyd giving her a "shot". I remember thinking, "What's wrong with this lady, and who is this Mother Boyd that's giving shots to people?" I was intrigued enough to go and see what it was all about, and eventually I did.

My first time going to the Fellowship Meetings was unforgettable. Elder Kenneth Collins preached the word, and after he finished preaching, Mother Estella Boyd got up and began laying hands on different individuals. I had never witnessed that kind of power before, so I was afraid. At the end of the service, I was introduced to her, and she looked at me and said, "Ask God to take away fear." When I got to my room that night, I prayed and asked God to take away fear. The next night, Mother Boyd prayed for me, and it felt like my insides were on fire. I didn't know exactly what happened to me when she laid hands on me, but I knew something happened. It felt like electricity enveloped my body. I understood that night what a "shot" was.

I was out for the rest of the service and awakened by someone rubbing my hand. It was Mother Stacks. She looked me in my eyes and said, "Mother gave you a good shot tonight. When you get to your room, you're going to feel sick and will probably be in the bathroom most of the night. Let God finish cleaning you up and filling you up with more of Him."

That night when I got to my room, it happened exactly like she said. I felt so loved and excited about Jesus! Every fourth weekend, I traveled to Detroit, Michigan to be in service. Mother Boyd laid hands on me each time I came. After the service, I would purchase the cassette tape and listen to it in the mornings on my way to work and in the evenings before bed until the next fourth weekend service. The word of God was quickening and making things alive down on the inside.

The more I traveled to Detroit for the Fellowship services, the more "shots" I received from Mother Estella Boyd. Each shot took off another layer of bondage. Things that once held me bound were broken off me when Mother Boyd prayed for me. My eyes became opened, and I was no longer held captive by the opinions of men. Mother Boyd would call me up many times after the service, and one of those times she said, "Daughter, God is going to grow you up quick in the spirit." That had been a prayer of mine, and God answered and continues to do so.

After some time, Mother Stacks began reaching out to me at the end of the services. One evening, she came to where I was sitting and started talking to me. I would see her when she and Mother Boyd came to Gary, Indiana for Fellowship meetings, and she would always talk to me after the service. I invited Mother Stacks to come to Chicago, and after much coaxing, she came.

At the time, I was living in Westmont, Illinois, so I put her in a hotel 5 minutes from my house. The night I was to take her to the airport, she decided to stay until the next morning and stayed at my home. I was so nervous! That's how our friendship began. I thought that's how our friendship would remain, but God had other plans.

HIS LOVE ENDURES FOREVER

My dad passed away on December 2, 1994, and I had all kinds of emotions bottled up inside when he died. In June of 1996, Mother Gertrude Stacks came to Chicago and ministered at Progressive Life-Giving Word Cathedral in Maywood, Illinois. When they put Mother Stacks up, she was ready. She preached a message entitled "Holiness, without which no man shall see the Lord." Every question I had before God, she answered. I was sitting on the edge of my seat and holding on to every word she spoke.

Mother Stacks preached on Galatians 5:19-21, "Now the works of the flesh are manifest, which are these; adultery, fornication, uncleanness, lasciviousness, idolatry, witchcraft, hatred, variance, emulations, wrath, strife, seditions, heresies, envyings, murders, drunkenness, revellings, and such like: of the which I tell you before, as I have also told you in time past, that they which do such things shall not inherit the kingdom of God. She said even though you might not be doing it, your flesh is capable of it." Whew!

She then went to Psalm 63:1-7, "O God, thou art my God; early will I seek thee: my soul thirsteth for thee, my flesh longeth for thee in a dry and thirsty land, where no water is; To see thy power and thy glory, so as I have seen thee in the sanctuary." Be-

27

cause thy lovingkindness is better than life, my lips shall praise thee. Thus will I bless thee while I live: I will lift up my hands in thy name. My soul shall be satisfied as with marrow and fatness; and my mouth shall praise thee with joyful lips. When I remember thee upon my bed, and meditate on thee in the night watches. Because thou hast been my help, therefore in the shadow of thy wings will I rejoice. One of the things Mother Stacks said was: "Seek God, and when you get down to the 10th day and that 11th day of seeking God, don't give up; persevere." Another thing she said was, "Open your mouth and tell God how you feel about things."

Immediately after the service, I ran downstairs to the tape table and bought two cassette tapes. When I came back upstairs, I went up to Mother Stacks and introduced myself. I told her how the message resonated with me. She grabbed my hands in hers and asked me my name. I told her, and she said, "I'm going to pray for you." When I got home from the service, I put the tape in my tape recorder and listened to it. I listened to that cassette tape day in and day out. In December 1996, the tape broke, so I immediately put the second one in that I had purchased and continued listening and obeying the word preached. When my dad died, there were so many things pent up inside of me because of things I went through as a child and teenager. I began talking out loud to God and telling Him how I felt about things. I needed answers to questions that had bombarded my mind for years.

On January 1, 1997, at 2:00 a.m., I poured my heart out to God. I remember saying, "God, you claim to be this loving Father, and I'm 36 years old and don't know what the love of a Father is." The Lord said, "Rita, I love you, and I'm your Father." I said, "That's what you're saying, but I don't know what that feels like." At that moment, Jesus came into my room. I was lying in my bed on my right side, and Jesus came into my room and rocked me in His arms. I wept so hard that I began purging. Jesus took a bath towel and held it under my mouth. After I filled that one, he held out another one, and I filled that one. After that, the Spirit said to me, "Since thou wast precious, I have loved thee with an everlasting love" (Isaiah 43:4). I remember crying and falling asleep in His arms.

I woke up at 6:30 a.m. that morning and looked around my room. I looked at the rocking chair in my room, and there were the two bath towels folded in the chair. There were no bath towels in my room that night, and I began weeping again. I got out of bed and went into the bathroom. When I looked in the mirror, I jumped back because my complexion was two shades brighter. That experience of the love of Jesus changed the trajectory of my life forever. It got rid of low self-esteem from words spoken over me that were not of God. It gave me a freedom in Christ I had never experienced before and didn't know I needed. I now knew what love felt like, and it was everything I needed to live my life fully for Christ.

I remember searching the internet and came across a document that was titled, "Love Letter From God." I read the letter, and it solidified everything that transpired! Here is a portion of it, and I hope it blesses you as much as it blessed me:

My beautiful child, whom I love so much. I know everything about you. I know when you sit down and when you stand up; I know what you do and when you do it. I am familiar with all your ways – every hair on your head is numbered. You were made perfectly in My image. I knew you and loved you before you were formed in your mother's womb. You were never a mistake as all your days are written in the Book of Life.

You must know, Child, you are fearfully and wonderfully made. I brought you forth on the day you were born. Take caution, though, as I have been misrepresented by those who don't know me. I am not some distant and angry Father. I am near you always...with you wherever you go. I am the complete expression of a loving Father, and it's my deepest desire to lavish more love and grace on you. I am your provider, and I will meet your every need through faith. My plan for your future is filled with purpose, an everlasting hope, love, peace, and joy. My thoughts towards you are as countless as the seashore sand. Trust Me, trust My Words, trust that you are My treasured possession.

My Child, if you seek Me with all your heart, you will find me. Delight yourself in Me, and I will give you the desires of your heart. I am your greatest encourager, the Father Who comforts you in all your troubles. Just as a shepherd carries his lamb, so have I carried you.

I am your Father, and I love you even as I love my Son, Jesus. It is in Jesus My love for you is revealed. Return to me daily. I have always been your loving Father, and I always will be.

In 2013, my mother's legs were not as strong as they used to be, so she spent most of her days sitting in her recliner doing word search puzzles or lying down. Her birthday was October 30th, and the family would always spend her birthdays with her at her house. Many times, my mother would call me to the house when she had things on her heart. I would go to her house, and we'd talk about the things that concerned her, and God always answered her. One of those times, my mother let me know that she was preparing to meet Jesus. She told me that she wanted me to eulogize her, and I said, "Mom, I can't do that. She said, "Punkin, you know momma." What could I say?

On my mother's 87th birthday, I went to her house, and my siblings, nieces, nephews, and a few of my great nieces and nephews were at the house. I spoke to everyone, kissed my mother, and gave her the gift I had for her. When I kissed her, the Lord said, "This will be your last family get-together with your mother." I went in the kitchen and sat in the chair with my back to the family. Tears ran down my face, and I couldn't stop them. My oldest sister came into the kitchen and asked what was wrong, and I asked her to please lower her voice. November 14th, a few weeks later, my mother went home to be with

Jesus. That was a pain I can't describe, but God is a lifter of every bowed-down head.

When my mother died, the Lord spoke to me and said, "There isn't a church that can hold the people because of the work your mother has done." The day of her funeral, people from all over traveled near and far to be at her service. Many were turned away because there was no more room in the church. I asked God to take me above the grief and let me eulogize her from the spirit realm. God did just that. He spoke about who she was and how she lived as a servant of the Lord Jesus Christ. Everything about her brought glory to God.

A YEAR OF OBEDIENCE THROUGH PAIN

After the vulgar comment incident at the COG-IC church, I began asking God if I could leave that church. Things got so bad that I would get depressed prior to going to church. I didn't understand why God would not allow me to leave. Time progressed, and I had to trust that God knew what He was doing with my life.

In my pursuit for the more of Jesus, I started waking up at 2:00 a.m. in the morning to demons being in my room. I remember the first night it happened like it was yesterday. I yelled Jesus and jumped out of bed, and turned on the light. I was afraid. I asked God, "Why would you let demons show up in my room"? His response was, "In order to cast out demons, you have to know demons." My God!

It was an intense journey, but God was with me. I was sitting in church one Sunday, and all of a sudden, the Minister of Music looked like one of the demons I had to whip in the Spirit. I tried to bust out the back of the pew. I began silently pleading the blood of Jesus. Going through that course prepared me for where God was taking me.

In the summer of 1997, while still attending the COGIC church, the Pastor's wife had her women's day program. Pastors and ministers' wives from all over came to be in the service that afternoon. The

33

service started, and we marched into the choir stand. The Minister of Music asked everyone to stand and said, "Now we'll have prayer by Sister Rita Newell." It caught me off guard because normally, whoever would participate on program would be given notice. After she said it, she bowed her head and began to laugh.

On my way to the podium, I said, "God, be with me." I prayed, Father God in the Name of Jesus, and I felt my spirit go up on what seemed like an elevator, and I prayed from that place in the Spirit. I then felt my spirit come back down and heard myself say, "And it is so by the power of the almighty God, in Jesus Name. Amen!" When I turned to go back to my seat, I heard in my right ear what sounded like an explosion. Right after that, the power of God enveloped that church. Everything that had breath began praising God. The Minister of Music got so mad that she wouldn't play the organ. The Pastor got off the piano, walked over to the organ and yelled at her to play the organ. The drummer kept playing.

Then, every time the first lady tried to continue with the service, one of the mothers would yell hallelujah, and the praises would begin all over again. The praise continued for 45 minutes. I just kept saying, God, I thank you! At the end of the service, the Pastor's daughter-in-law said, "I don't know where you've been, but keep going and doing what you're doing because I see God all over you." If God be for us, who can be against us (Romans 8:31).

While in the Chorale, we had annual concerts. Each member of the Chorale would invite their friends and families to come out and enjoy a night of praise. We were well known in Chicago as one of the best groups in the city. We traveled to different cities to sing praises to God. Our annual concerts were held each year in the month of September. We would rehearse two, sometimes three times a week, leading up to the concert.

In September 1997, I invited many people to come out to our annual concert, and 40 people showed up. That night, God anointed me to sing like never before. God's power was evident in the room. The more I experienced freedom in Christ, the angrier the devil got. I remember the night Mother Boyd shot me into the spirit realm, and the scales fell off my eyes. I saw for the first time what kind of church I was a part of. It was a very controlling and toxic environment. As long as those in position could control me, they were fine. Once God freed me and gave me a voice, those in position turned against me.

Months after the concert, the Minister of Music began having rehearsals on Tuesday nights, and everyone knew about the change except me. I would drive to the church on Wednesday nights for rehearsal, and there would be no one there. When one of the chorale members asked why I wasn't at rehearsal, I told her I wasn't aware of the change, and after it happened a few more times, I stopped showing up. I was actually glad that I didn't have to go to church and fight demons. Demons that I hadn't noticed in people before began manifesting and tried to speak damnation to my soul. I stood strong in what Jesus had done for me and would not be moved by any of it.

In November 1997, the Pastor's wife asked me to speak for Women's Day. She and the Pastor would be in Memphis, Tennessee, for the National Holy Convocation. I went to church that morning, and there weren't many people there. When I got up to speak, the Holy Spirit said, "Don't read your notes. I'm going to speak through you." I began speaking about some of my encounters with Jesus. God anointed me to speak his word with accuracy and boldness. When I finished my message, we praised God. People who had never praised God before praised God that Sunday.

December 28, 1997, was the last Sunday of the year. While I was sitting in church, the Holy Spirit said, "Hug everyone in here before you leave today, starting with your enemies." I said God, I can't do that. God said the same thing to me again. I said, "God, if you give me the strength, I'll do it." After church, I went and hugged the pastor, his wife, his oldest daughter, his second oldest daughter, and then the rest of the members.

The following Wednesday (December 31, 1997) was Watch Night service. I got a call from my Godfather, Bishop Jesse T. Stacks from Michigan, and he said, "Daughter, I was in prayer, and the Lord told me to tell you not to go to Watch Night service." I obeyed, and on New Year's Day, I drove to Indiana for a spa trip. I went and had a spa service and returned to my room. When I returned to my room, the Holy Spirit started singing, "The peace that passeth all understanding, shall keep your hearts and minds through Christ Jesus." I immediately got down on my knees next to the bed and began weeping. The Holy Spirit spoke to me and said, "This day I have released thee from the Church of God in Christ." I got up off my knees and praised my God.

When I returned home from my spa trip, I typed up my resignation letter and mailed it. I got a call from Bishop Stacks again, and he said, "Daughter, I was in prayer, and the Lord told me to tell you don't go to church tomorrow night; it's a setup. When I got home Friday from work, the pastor had left a voicemail on my answering machine. He asked that I come to church to meet with him and his wife to talk about my resignation. As far as I was concerned, it was finished, so I deleted the voicemail and never looked back. "For I know the plans I have for you, declares the LORD, plans to prosper you and not to harm you, plans to give you hope and a future" (Jeremiah 29:11). There's safety in Jesus!

After God released me from my church, I began going to Prayer Tower Church in Gary, Indiana, where Elder Kenneth R. Collins was the Pastor. Elder Collins reminded me of the scriptures I had read about John the Baptist. He lived out Matthew 3:3 – "The voice of one crying in the wilderness. Prepare ye the way of the Lord, make his paths straight. He preached holiness without which no man shall see the Lord." Hebrews 12:14

Elder Collins was affectionately known as Dick Tracy. He would say, "I'm Dick Tracy, and I'm here to make a bust." He was known for dissecting a lie and revealing the truth. If a demon manifested in his services, he would cast the devil out. He loved singing praises to God prior to preaching, and when he was done preaching, God demonstrated his power immediately following the message. He would always say, "That yes got to come down in your belly"!

Years later, I moved on in ministry, but I would often come and see Elder Collins. One day in prayer, God told me to go and check on Elder Collins. Sunday after church, I drove out to Gary, Indiana, and was in service with Elder Collins. After the service was over, I got a chance to speak with him. I relayed the message that God had given me for him, and 11 days later, Elder Collins went home to be with the Lord. I'm so grateful that I obeyed God and I got a chance to see him prior to his transition. God is so faithful!

MY JOURNEY OF HEALING

In 1982, I was in my car driving to the train station and stumbled upon Kenneth E. Hagin teaching on the radio from 6:30 a.m. to 7:00 a.m. I enjoyed his message so much that I would listen to it every morning. In the summer of 1984, a few of my sisters in Christ (Debra, Bonnie, and Pam) traveled to Tulsa, Oklahoma, to be in Kenneth E. Hagin's Camp Meeting services. At that time, Dad Hagin's services were being held in the auditorium of Oral Roberts University. We got there Saturday afternoon and visited the biblical gardens at the University. You could literally feel the presence of God on those grounds.

I asked God to heal me in the service because I was dealing with injuries I sustained in a bad car accident months prior when I was hit by a drunk driver. My sisters in Christ and I checked into our hotel rooms, got dressed, and came back for the service that evening. Dad Hagin preached on the healing power of God. After he concluded his message, he called for people who needed to be healed to come down to the front. I immediately got out of my seat and went down to the front. I was placed by one of his team members in the front of the center aisle. I was standing there thanking God for my healing when another one of the team members came and moved me towards the back. I said in my spirit, God, let him take me right back to where I was standing. The team member came back and moved me back to the front, where I was standing.

When Dad Hagin came off the podium, he prayed for the people who came down to the front, and when he came up to me, he put his fingertips very lightly on both sides of my face, and I fell out under the power of God. I knew instantly that I was healed. That was the first time I actually witnessed the healing power of God. My heart was full of thanksgiving. Hebrews 4:15 – "For we have not a high priest which cannot be touched with the feeling of our infirmities. . ." He's such a tangible God!

In May 1999, Mother Boyd came to Gary, Indiana, to be in service. She was 84 years old at the time. The service was held at this small church called Upper Room. The church was packed with people coming to experience God's miraculous power. That night, I was videotaping the service, and Mother Boyd was sitting in her seat. She had on a purple and gold robe with the matching hat. She would motion for different ones to come to her, and they would bow down in front of her, and she would pray for them. I said in my spirit, God, don't forget about me.

At that time, I was dealing with fibroids and painful menstrual cycles. Just as I said that, Mother Boyd asked her nurse to get the video camera from me and called me over to her. I got down on my knees in front of her, and she blew in my face. Next, she laid hands on my head. She took her hand and put it towards my back on my right side. She gently slid her hand from my back to the front of my stomach. The best way I can describe it is it felt like things pulling on the inside of my stomach.

When she finished praying for me, my stomach looked like I was seven months pregnant. However, everything was shifted to the right side. I was out for the rest of the service. I remember having to be driven home that night, and as I lay on my bed, God showed me laying on an operating table, and Mother Boyd was suspended in the air on my right side looking down at me.

Mother Boyd put her hand on the top of my stomach as I lay on the table and said, "God, do it now!" Afterwards, what looked like a big red ball came out of me, and the vision ended. God told me the action of Mother Boyd's hand connected the fibroids on the inside and outside of my uterus into one big fibroid, and all my doctor had to do was open me up and lift it out.

After that experience, I was drunk in the spirit for three days and couldn't speak in English. After I came around, I noticed that my stomach was hard. At that time, Bishop Stacks was not feeling well, so Mother Stacks didn't make it to that service. I called Mother Stacks and let her know what happened in the service and that my stomach felt hard and wouldn't go down. She told me to go to the doctor and let them check me out. I went to see my doctor, and when she examined me, she said, "I think it's cancer. I shouted out of my mouth, " It's not cancer." She then said, " Maybe it's your liver." I shouted again, "It's not my liver." DEATH and LIFE are in the power of YOUR TONGUE!

Afterwards, my doctor made an appointment for me to see my gynecologist. When I went to see her, she examined me and said it was a massive fibroid. She said I would have to have a myomectomy, which is a surgical procedure to remove noncancerous growths in the uterus. She explained that it would be a very bloody surgery, and I said right after her words, "God, don't let there be much blood at all." She said, "I'll have to give you a blood transfusion." I said, "God, no blood transfusion." She said I'll have to give you a hysterectomy. I said, "God, no hysterectomy."

When I left the doctor's office, I said, "God, I know you didn't start this process not to complete it, so I trust you." I had gone through so much in my walk with Christ and was very intimidated by people in leadership positions. Many used their positions as a tool to control and manipulate me, but God kept my mind through all of it. The Lord spoke to me and said, "With that tumor, I'm going to take out intimidation and replace it with my boldness." I asked God to please let His Spirit be keener in me than it's ever been, and He did.

My surgery was scheduled for August 16, 1999. My mother spent the night with me, and we went to the hospital early Monday morning. I was prepped for surgery and given anesthesia. The next thing I remember is seeing Mother Boyd in that Purple and Gold robe with the matching hat, smiling down at me and saying, "Daughter, it's over!" I came out of the anesthesia right then and was taken to my room. I was in so much pain that the doctor had me on a morphine drip. I was in and out of sleep, and a little while later, Dr. Connie came into the room and started calling my name.

I said, "God, I need to know what you did for me through my doctor's mouth." She said, Rita, that was one of the easiest surgeries I've ever performed. I said, "Thank you, Jesus." She said, "There was hardly any blood." I replied, "Thank you, Jesus." She said, "I didn't have to transfuse you," and I said, "Thank you, Jesus." She said, "I didn't have to take your uterus," and I said, "Thank you, Jesus."

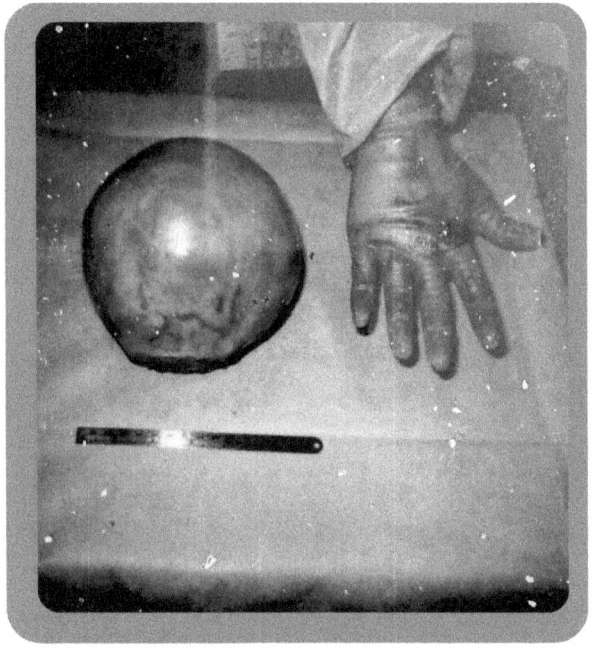

Dr. Connie gave me three pictures of the tumor that she removed, and I kept one, gave one to my mother, and gave one to Mother Boyd. When I gave

Mother Boyd her picture, she quickened and almost fell backwards. While I was recuperating, I asked God to tell Mother Boyd how much I love her. I promised God that I would sow a $300 seed in Mother Boyd's life every month as long as she had breath in her body. I wasn't trying to pay her for praying for me. I was grateful for her unselfish love towards God's people. She wanted nothing but God's best for His people looking for nothing in return, and I was happy to sow into her. God is involved in every aspect of our lives. He's a miracle-working God!

I was released from the hospital on the evening of August 18th. My sister Rosie came to the hospital to take me home. I was up most of the night in pain. I had staples from the top of my stomach to the bottom of it. The next day, my friend Rita left work early to come and sit with me and my friend Jackie came over Friday evening and stayed three nights with me. Because of the staples, I had to sleep sitting up, so I slept on my chaise. Around 2:30 a.m. Saturday morning, I awakened to what felt like someone choking me. Jackie was lying on my sofa, snoring. I kept trying to say Jesus, but nothing happened. I whispered, Jackie, please plead the blood of Jesus.

The Holy Spirit woke her up, and she pleaded the blood of Jesus with authority. It felt like something broke off my neck. She went right back to sleep, and tears rolled down my face. I asked, "God, why did you let a demon come into my home and choke me?" The Lord said, "I have made thee a prophet likened unto Samuel. So much so that people will ask are you here for peace or war. He said, "As long as you stay before me, not a word you speak will fall to the ground." The Lord continued, "My people don't fear me and I'm bringing judgment back to the household of faith. Preachers are going to get up to preach and fall down dead in the pulpit, and in hell they will lift up their eyes." I cried bitter tears that night.

Saturday morning, when Jackie awakened, she asked why I asked her to plead the blood of Jesus. I explained what happened to her, and she was like OMG! After getting up to take a pain pill, my sisters Charlotte and Tarrie and my friend Rita came over to see me. My sisters went to go get food to ensure I ate something and spent the day with me. The next day, Elder Collins and two of the brothers from the church came to see me. Elder Collins ministered and prayed for me. The healing process took about three months, but it was time well spent with Jesus.

A month after my surgery, I received a call from Mother Boyd. She stated that she was going to be in Savannah, Georgia in October 1999 for a service and wanted me to come. I wasn't fully healed, but my doctor cleared me for the trip with restrictions. I flew down with one of the sisters from church, and we got to the service late the first night. Mother Boyd was waiting for me to come through the door, and as soon as I sat down, she had me to come up to the front of the church and testify. I could hardly get the words out of my mouth without crying because I was so grateful for God's mercy towards me.

The next night, Mother Boyd had the usher to sit me on the front row. After the word of God was preached, she charged some of her ministers to go and pray for the people. Sis. Bea Padillo came and prayed for me. After prayer, Mother Boyd told Sis. Bea and one of the other ministers to bring me to her so she could pray for me. Sis. Bea told Mother Boyd she had already prayed for me. Mother Boyd reiterated, " Bring her to me."

My incision from the surgery wasn't fully healed. When Bea and the other sister came to get me, the other sister popped me in my stomach where the incision was, and I was bent over in excruciating pain. When they took me to Mother Boyd, Mother Boyd rebuked the sister sharply and told her to go and sit down. I sat down next to Mother Boyd in tears, and she blew in my face and prayed over every place that Sis. Bea had prayed. She took her fingertips and gently touched my incision, and all the pain left immediately. Thank you, Jesus!

Sis. Bea took me back to my seat, and I closed my eyes and was in the spirit realm. After the service, I had to be carried to the car, and my sister put me in bed, shoes and all. I came down at 3:00 a.m., and my sister and the other sister were in the living room talking. I went into the living room and told them I wanted a hamburger. I wasn't a big hamburger person, so I thought it strange that I had a taste for one. We went through a drive-through and came back to our hotel suite. They went to their rooms and went to bed.

I stayed up in the living room because I had questions about what the Lord showed me while in the spirit realm. I waited until 5:00 a.m. and called Mother Stacks. Bishop answered the phone, and I apologized for calling so early. I told him I really needed to speak to Mother Stacks and heard her tell him that she'll take the call in the living room. When she answered the phone, I asked her if God shows you graphic things in the spirit. She said yes. I shared with her what I saw, and she said, "Well, Mother Boyd has her answer. I'll have to tell her later on. I couldn't believe it. Mother Boyd wanted to know the truth about the situation, so she shot me in the spirit realm to give her the answer.

The last night was considered our blast off service. The spirit of praise was in the room. People sang and testified about God's goodness. After the service ended, Mother Boyd asked Elder Collins to bring me to her. When I sat down, she said, "Daughter, God told me, I'm going to work a miracle through your hands for someone that really loves you, and God told me how much you love me, and I love you too."

She then said, "God also told me that you will help take care of me. Tears rolled down my face, and today, I'm still blown away about how deeply involved God is in our lives. All we have to do is acknowledge Him in all our ways. When I left Savannah, Georgia, I went back to work a few weeks later. Every month, I sent $300 to Mother Stacks to give to Mother Boyd, and she did so and let her know it was from me. I completed my promise to God, and I'm grateful for the privilege to do so.

THIS SICKNESS IS NOT UNTO DEATH

My Godmother, Dr. Gertrude Stacks, transitioned from this life to eternity on September 20, 2021. After her death, a spirit of depression was working overtime to overtake me. I prayed constantly for it to lift, and it was a struggle. I was a board member of my Godmother's church, and when she passed, she left no succession plan in place, so there was a lot of confusion. Everybody wanted the church, even those who were never called to pastor. I asked the Lord if I could resign from the board, and He said, "Not yet."

We continued having board meetings to ensure Dr. Stacks' funeral arrangements and the church's business was intact. After Dr. Stacks funeral services were over, things transpired, and I found myself being overwhelmed with things relating to Shalom. My time spent with God after she passed was spent in conversations about the church and the issues surrounding it. It felt like it was a struggle to get my mind back totally on the things of God.

In December 2021, I wasn't feeling well, and Covid was at an all-time high. Rita and Alice came by to check on me, and I did a video call with the doctor. She called in my prescription, and they picked it up and brought it back to me. Days passed, and I got worse. The following Thursday, Alice came to my house, and it startled me when I heard her inside the house. She said, Re, put your phone on the charger. Friday and Saturday are still a blur. The devil was trying to take me out.

Sunday afternoon on December 12, 2021, Alice came back to the house, and I was lying in bed. She knew I needed medical attention so she called 911 so I could go to the hospital. The ambulance came and Alice followed the ambulance to Christ Hospital. I was in and out of consciousness, but God was with me. He would wake me up and let me speak when it was necessary to do so. I heard the nurse telling Alice she had to leave. I heard Alice tell the nurse, I'm not leaving until you put her in a room.

While unconscious in the natural, I was conscious in the spirit realm. I remember being face down on wet, cold concrete, and the Lord telling me to come out of futility. I know now that futility can come from a range of root causes: someone's not in the right role, or is going through a tough personal battle that shifts their focus from God, or maybe they've been made to feel like they don't matter. While not totally understanding futility at the time, I remember repenting to God.

I wasn't aware that I had taken on things pertaining to Shalom that had nothing to do with me. I had Covid, and after about 22 hours, a nurse came and took me to a room on the Covid floor, and Alice left the hospital. The worst part of being in the hospital during Covid was that none of your family members could come to the hospital to visit you. The first three days, I moaned in pain. I don't know if it came from the sickness itself or from the medication the hospital administered. Some of the nurses were nice, and some were not. My sister Rosie called the hospital daily to ensure I was being taken care of.

The evening of Christmas Eve, the night shift nurse came in with her iPad and asked if I wanted her to FaceTime my family so I could see them. I knew everyone was at my niece Tawana's house, so I said "yes." I was still weak, but I was so grateful to see my family members. My sisters didn't take it well to see me in that state, but God was with me. On December 30th, the hospital decided to discharge me. A nurse came in with a walker to ensure I could make it to the restroom. After having me walk back and forth from the bed to the restroom, I was sent home that evening in a non-emergency ambulance.

I came home with a walker and the following day, I received an oxygen tank. My sister Rose and her daughter Jontae were waiting for me when I arrived home. Rose stayed with me and took care of me while I was recuperating. She ensured I ate, took my medicine, and walked in the house on my walker. Tae would stay on the weekends and change my linens and clean my bathrooms. My sisters would cook food and bring it to the house. After a few weeks, I began physical therapy, and once completed, I had acupuncture to ensure my lungs were clear.

That experience put me back in true fellowship with God. I thank God for His unconditional love, His grace, and His mercy that He's always extended to me. Once the people of Shalom selected someone to pastor the church, I asked him to remove me from the board. Forgetting those things which are behind and reaching forward to those things which are ahead. I press toward the mark for the prize of the high calling of God in Christ Jesus (Philippians 3:13-14).

CHANGING OF THE GUARDS

Bishop Stacks passed away on October 3, 2001, and Mother Stacks became the Pastor of Shalom church. She later changed the name of the church to Shalom Fellowship International church. After his funeral, Mother Stacks asked that I stay for a week to assist her with some legalities concerning the church. I began traveling to Detroit, Michigan every weekend to be in service with Mother Stacks.

Some Sundays after church, we would go and eat dinner and stop by Mother Boyd's house. I would go into Mother Boyd's bedroom and sit at the foot of her bed. She would speak words of wisdom, and I would listen intently. One Sunday after church, Mother Boyd asked me where I went to church. I replied I went to Mother's church. She asked, "What did she teach?" I replied, "She taught Can You Hold God's Secrets".

Mother Boyd, then asked with interest, "What did she say?" I said, "She said there is a certain place in the spirit realm that God will reveal secrets to you that are not even written in the bible." Mother Boyd quickened on the bed and said, "Sho you right". I looked at her and said, "You bad Mother Boyd!"

Months passed, and one Sunday evening, Mother Stacks called me and said, "Mother is talking about taking a trip out of here, so you should come down and see her. Don't bring anyone with you." I agreed and came down that Friday evening. Mother Stacks picked me up from the airport, and on Saturday morning, we went to breakfast.

After breakfast, we stopped by the church, and Mother Stacks began showing me all the renovations she was making to the church. We were upstairs in the sanctuary, and Mother Stacks told me her plans for the church. All of a sudden, she turned her head to the right like someone called her and said, "Mother just summoned me in the spirit. We have to go."

We left Shalom and went to Mother Boyd's house. We arrived at Mother Boyd's home at 11:30 a.m. Her daughter Hattie opened the door, and we went into Mother Boyd's bedroom. She was waiting on Mother Stacks when we walked in. Mother Stacks hugged her, and I hugged her. Mother Stacks pulled a chair up next to Mother Boyd's bed, and Mother Boyd went straight into the spirit realm.

Mother Boyd was in and out of the spirit realm for about four hours. I was seated near the back of her bedroom, taking it all in. When Mother Boyd stopped going into the spirit realm, Mother Stacks said, "Alright, Mother. We're getting ready to go," and she stood up and moved her chair back to where it was. When she went to hug Mother Boyd, Mother Boyd grabbed Mother Stacks' hand very hard and wouldn't let it go. I got up and put the chair next to Mother Boyd's bed, and Mother Stacks sat back down.

I asked God, "What's going on" while she's holding Mother Stack's hand. The Lord said, "Mother Boyd is ensuring that everything is well while she's preparing to meet me." Mother Boyd loosened her grip on Mother Stack's hand at 7:30 p.m. We got ready to leave, and Mother Stacks left out of the room. I went over to Mother Boyd and kissed her on her forehead. I asked, "Are you getting ready to leave me?"

She said, "Daughter, I'm getting ready to top that flight." I said, "Did you pray for me?" She said, "Yes, have you been feeling pain in your right side?" I said, "Yes, ma'am." She replied, "I know you have. You have to be in pain and labour to bring forth, O daughter of Zion, like a woman in travail" (Micah 4:10).

Two weeks later, I went to Detroit, Michigan, to be in service Saturday afternoon and Sunday morning with Mother Stacks. While we were in service Saturday afternoon, we received word that Mother Boyd had passed. I will always cherish the private moments I had with Mother Boyd, and I remained faithful in my giving until Mother Boyd closed her eyes on April 5, 2003. I truly thank God for every "shot" into the spirit realm and every impartation I received from her.

MY JOURNEY OF FAITH

In February 2003, the Lord spoke to me and said, "Rita, I must teach you how to trust me." I replied, "God, I do trust you." He said, "No, you don't; you trust that paycheck you get twice a month". That statement from God marked the beginning of my faith walk. May 2003, I got downsized from my job at the law firm I was working for. I received severance pay from the company and collected unemployment for six months. During the time I was unemployed, I continued sending out resumes, but nothing came through. I would ask God why job opportunities weren't opening up for me, and it seemed as if all of heaven was quiet. My soul was in anguish because I couldn't hear God.

Things got really tight as far as my living expenses were concerned. There was nothing left financially that I could count on. There were many days that I didn't have my daily necessities. There were days that I didn't have food to eat. I began getting eviction notices, repossession notices, and shut-off notices.

One day, I got tired of crying about not having any money to meet my daily needs. I said, "God, if you let me get evicted and they put my furniture outside on the front lawn and let the bank repossess my car, so be it. I'm done, and I will just tell people that this God that I've been talking about all these years couldn't take care of me."

What I love about God is that when you speak your heart, He doesn't hold it against you. I had been in control of my life without trusting God fully and wasn't even aware of it. God had to teach me how to relinquish control and fully trust Him with all of me.

After my conversation with God, I received a phone call from Verizon Wireless because my cell phone bill was two months behind. When I answered the phone, the representative told me due to nonpayment, they had to cut off my phone because my phone bill was delinquent. I understood, and she forwarded my call to the department that handles cut-offs. When the lady answered the phone, she said, "Rita, I've pulled up your account, and I see where you've made all your payments on time. Is there something going on?"

I was still in tears from my conversation with God, but I let her know that I was unemployed. I told her this was my only means of communication, and if Verizon cut my phone off, I couldn't receive calls from any temp agencies. The lady put me on hold, and when she got back on the phone, she said, "Rita, I've just reversed your balance out of the system. She also gave me a two-month credit. I cried so hard, but I was able to thank her through my tears. She said, "I was unemployed last year, so I understand. I'll be praying for you, Rita. I knew that the lady I spoke to was an angel.

My oldest sister Gemilla had accepted Jesus Christ as her personal savior recently, and she called me that afternoon. She asked me how much my car note was and what the name of the finance company was. I told her, and she called me back a little while later and said, "Lift your head up, girl. I just paid those two car notes." I couldn't do anything but cry because I knew God was at work.

After I got off the phone with my sister, my friend Melody called me. She asked if she could stop by my home after work, and I said, "sure." That evening, she rang my doorbell, and when I opened the door, she came in with bags of groceries. She came in with bags of food that she had cooked for me. It was such an emotional day.

When I went upstairs to my bedroom, I kept thanking God for all He had done for me. I knew that if He did that, He would take care of my rent. Early the next morning, my God sister Alice rang my doorbell. When I answered the door, Alice came in with my eviction notice in her hand. She said, "Re, I just paid your rent." I fell backwards on my Chaise and cried. It felt like a huge weight was lifted off my shoulders. I was always the one who always blessed people, and when I was at my lowest, God used His people to bless me. Things went well financially for a while, but things eventually ended up where they were.

THE STACKS CHRONICLES

The night Mother Stacks stayed at my home marked the beginning of a Godmother/Goddaughter relationship. She picked up from where Mother Boyd left off as far as shots into the spirit realm and spiritual impartations were concerned. I traveled every weekend to Detroit for a few years until God told me to come off the road and go to Pastor Bill Winston's church. The Lord said, "Your next level of faith is in his mouth." I obeyed and began growing in my faith walk. Whenever there were special services at Shalom, I made sure I traveled to be in those services. I was christened as a Daughter of Zion in one of those services.

Even though Mother Stacks pastored Shalom, she continued traveling to different cities, teaching God's word with signs following the word that was taught. I traveled with her for many years. A lot of times, after the services, she would be exhausted and would travel back to Chicago with me to rest. God used my home as a place of refuge for Mother Stacks for almost 25 years. The Lord taught me many things while serving Mother Stacks, and I had to learn quickly. A lot of people who were in her circle began talking against her to me, and when I stopped them, they turned against me.

There was a time when one of my sisters in Christ and I went to Detroit one Saturday morning to be in service with Mother Stacks on Sunday. My sister in Christ was pastoring a church at the time, so she met with Mother Stacks that Saturday evening to discuss church stuff. She had ulterior motives and said many terrible things about the members and I. The Holy Spirit told me what happened, so I went to my hotel room and asked God to show me how to deal with the situation. When I got back to Chicago, things began to unfold, and there were many lies that she had spoken against me. She blamed Mother Stacks for all the things she said, and things went left quickly. I spent the next three nights after work wrapped up in my prayer blanket in the middle of my bedroom floor, asking God to please heal my heart.

I ended my association with the sister and spoke to Mother Stacks and asked her to lose my number and never call me again. In the wee hours of Saturday morning, I felt the pain in my heart being pulled out. The Holy Spirit said, "Get up and get in bed." At 5:00 a.m., the Holy Spirit woke me up and said, "Go take your shower". I did, and when I was done, I sat in my chair next to my bed and began talking to God and reading my bible. At 5:55 a.m., the Holy Spirit said, "Your Godmother is going to call you at 6:00 o'clock, and when she does, I want you to repent." I didn't understand, so I enquired of God. He said, "When you told her lose your number and don't ever call you again, you stirred up old wounds in her heart." At 6:00 a.m., she called me, and I obeyed the Holy Spirit. That incident gave us time to have a heart-to-heart with each other and agree to respect each other's boundaries.

God used me to care for His vessel after Bishop Stacks death, and He gave me the capacity to obey His commands. I got a chance to be up close and personal with one of God's generals in the Spirit, and at times, it wasn't easy. She was a powerful woman of God, but the Holy Spirit dealt with me about her humanity. A lot of times, when God uses a person in powerful ways, if we're not careful, we'll get caught up in the way God uses a person and forget that they're human.

Mother Stacks knew she was safe in my home and she could trust me. She would tell me often how she enjoyed being in my home not only to rest, but that she could be herself. She had a great sense of humor and loved God with all her heart. There were times when she would be in her room and not come out for days because she was fasting and praying. She loved serving God and His people.

In May 2005, I received a call from my Mother Stacks asking that I come to the Daughters of Zion Convention. I told her I would not attend because I wasn't working at that time and didn't have the funds to do so. She said I'll call you back. An hour later, she called and said, "I just put $250 in your account. Just get here, and I'll help you."

After I spoke to Mother Stacks, one of her members called me and asked if I was coming to the Daughters of Zion conference. I told her I wasn't working, and she said, "If you get here, you can stay with me, and I'll feed you." I didn't want to go, but the Holy Spirit led me to do so. I got there on Friday, and the conference started Friday night. The conference ended Sunday afternoon, and Monday morning, I got up to get on the road to come home. When I got ready to leave, my Godmother called me and asked what I was doing. I told her I was getting ready to get on the road to go home, but she convinced me to go to breakfast with her first. She picked me up, and we went to Steve's Deli in Bloomfield Hills, Michigan.

When we got to the restaurant, we were seated, and the waitress took our orders. When the waitress left the table, Mother Stacks pulled an envelope out of her purse. It was her offering from the Daughters of Zion conference. She looked at me and said, " How much is your rent and I said $929." She counted it out twice. She then asked, " How much is your car note and I said $424." She counted it out twice, and I put my head down on the table, crying profusely. I heard her saying, "I know you need money for your utilities; you need money for food; you need money for your toiletries and perfume; you need money for gas." She kept counting out money for me. With my head still down, I heard the waitress come back to the table and ask Mother Stacks if I was okay. Mother Stacks asked her to give us a few minutes.

When I was able to lift my head, I took my napkin to dry my face. I told her how much I appreciated what she did. She gave me all but $40 of her offering. She said, " Put this in your purse and take care of your bills when you get home." Before we left the restaurant, she said, "Rita, once you get home, God is going to give you a job." When I got home and counted the money, she had given me a little over $6,000.

GOD'S TIMING IS PERFECT

The next morning, I received a phone call from a temp agency. They asked if I could report to a law firm the next morning, and I agreed to do so. I worked temp for the company for five months, and the assignment ended. I prayed and asked God to give me a permanent position at the law firm. A month went by, and I called the HR Manager and told her I really needed a job. She said I'm working on it and in January 2006, I got called back to work an assignment and ended up as a permanent employee.

A position came up to work for one of the partners, and I applied for it. God blessed me to get the position, and things went well for a while. That same year, God blessed me to move into a brand-new tri-level townhome that I rented with the option to buy. It was everything that I desired and more. When my Godmother would visit, by the time she got to the third level, she would say, "Please let the next house not have as many stairs." I remember saying, "God, if there is such thing as a two-level townhouse, please give me one." What I love about God is that He remembers things we ask of Him, even when we forget.

The owner of the townhome had a hardwood flooring business. In 2008, he had to have major surgery and was no longer able to work. I paid my rent, and instead of paying the mortgage with it, he paid his daughter's college tuition. The townhome eventually went into foreclosure, and I had to move. One night, I woke up to go to the restroom, and the Lord spoke to me and said, "You ought to be tired of the devil pressing you out of your promises." I said, "God, I am." He said, "Then just as hard as the devil is trying to keep you from them, you have to be that much more determined to receive them." I remember telling God that I never wanted another house that wasn't built from the ground. I ended up putting my furniture in storage and had nowhere to go.

I called a friend, and she allowed me to stay with her for a few months. My cousin called while I was staying with my friend and offered me a room to rent at her home. I looked at some townhomes to buy, and God didn't allow any of my offers to be accepted. After six months of staying with my cousin, I left and moved to Lombard, IL, and rented a two-bedroom, two-bathroom Condo.

I felt so discouraged that I ended up paying rent instead of putting my money towards a mortgage. The day I moved into my Condo, I said, "God, I'm not asking you about a home anymore. When you're ready for me to have one, you let me know." Honestly, I was angry that God didn't allow any of my offers to be accepted, but I had forgotten what I said to God when I lost my townhome.

I moved into my Condo on May 1, 2010, and decided to make it my home. I asked God why He didn't let any of my offers on the houses I looked at go through. He replied, "You told me when you were losing your home that you didn't want another house that wasn't built from the ground." I repented to the Lord through tears because it was at that moment that I realized that God always wants His best for His children!

In December 2010, I got down in prayer, and before I could start praying, the Lord said, "Rita, I want you to go and look at that Townhouse in Chicago Ridge." I sat up and said, "God, what Townhouse in Chicago Ridge?" He said, "Get up and get on your computer." I turned on my computer and the Holy Spirit showed me where the townhouse was, and I called the number that was listed.

I made an appointment and met with the builder's agent at 1:00 p.m. She decided to show me a few models in Bridgeview, Illinois, and tried to get me to buy there. I asked if there was a townhome available in Chicago Ridge, and she replied yes, but it's the builder's model. I said that's the one I want to see. I followed her to the townhouse, and when I stepped inside the foyer, the Holy Spirit said, "This is your house." It was a corner lot two-level townhouse built from the ground with three bedrooms, three bathrooms, vaulted ceilings, and plenty of space.

Two weeks after looking at the townhouse, I got a call from the builder's agent, and she said, "Rita, I'm just calling to tell you that there are three contingent offers on the townhouse, and you will not be able to buy it." I told her that I didn't care if there were 300 offers: that's my townhouse. She said, "Whatever, I'm just calling to let you know." I said, "You will see that my God is God." She hung up, and I called her the next day and told her I would be there Saturday with my realtor to put my earnest money down.

The three offers that were on the townhouse, of course, fell through. I went into the office that Saturday with my realtor, and the Lord told me to make an offer of $195,000 for the property. The agent laughed at me and said, "He'll never go for that." I asked her if she was the builder or if she worked for the builder. Her response was, "I know he won't go for that." I said, "Call him and find out."

When she came back in the room, she said, "I can't believe this, but he said, you can have it for $197,000." The Lord said, "Tell her you'll take it." I did, and the Lord said, "Tell her you'll put down $1,000 today and bring the balance to the closing." She said the builder wouldn't go for that either, but he did. My bid was accepted, which gave me $92,000 off the asking price.

I was still renting my Condo, and my lease wasn't up until the end of May. My closing date on my townhouse was February 1st. I remember asking God to please not let me have to pay rent and a mortgage at the same time. Each time I was given a closing date, God would allow something to happen so that the closing couldn't take place. I closed on my new townhouse on March 31, 2011, and my first mortgage payment wasn't due until May 1st. I paid my last month's rent on my Condo on April 1st and had the entire month to get everything out and ensure everything was in order prior to my leaving. God is such a good Father.

When I moved into my townhouse, I got my blessed oil and anointed my home. I dispatched my guardian angels outside on both sides of my front door. God allowed me to see them in the spirit realm, so I knew they were there. After I moved in, Terrilyn came by to pick up something, and when she stepped into the foyer and began walking up the stairs, she was saying, " Ooh, ooh, it's prayer up in this house."

A week after I moved into my home, my God-mother drove to Chicago and got in around 9:00 p.m. The Holy Spirit told me she had arrived, so I went to the front door to let her in. When I opened the front door, she stepped to the side of the banister and said, "Oh, Jesus". It was like she bumped into something. When she stepped inside the foyer, she said, "Girl, you didn't tell me you had angels out here." I love it when God backs up the things that we request of Him.

OBEDIENCE IS BETTER THAN SACRIFICE

Mother Stacks would come to my home often to get much-needed rest. She was a mother to the body of Christ. If people were sick in Chicago, they'd call for her to come, and she would do so without hesitation. I would drive her to the homes of the sick and shut-in, and she would anoint them, pray for them, and God would raise them up. She shared a lot about her life with me. One day, she shared her testimony. She said she would drink and party every night, and she smoked three packs of cigarettes a day for eight solid years. She shared how God saved her at one of Mother Boyd's revival services and took the taste of alcohol and cigarettes from her mouth immediately.

About two months after her salvation, she told me that she wasn't feeling well, so she went to the doctor's office. When the doctor checked her, he asked her to leave his office because he didn't want her "dying in his office." Her blood had dropped so low that she was on the verge of death. She made it to church where Mother Boyd was, and when she sat down, her dad, who was a prophet, got up and said, "There's a dead woman in this church."

Mother Boyd asked two of the women to bring Mother Stacks up to the front where she was and sit her in the chair. When they sat her in the chair, she slipped out of the chair onto the floor. Mother Boyd had a voice that sounded like thunder, so when she called on the name of Jesus, Mother Stacks said it felt like she had gotten an electrical shock. God picked her up from the floor into a standing position and put victory in her feet. She danced and danced, and as she did, many people were delivered and set free. She said, "Right now, when God is going to deliver and set free, he'll let me dance first."

After church, Mother Stacks wanted to know what God had done, so she and her dad went to the hospital for them to check her blood. A spirit of joy hit her dad, and then it hit her, and they began laughing uncontrollably. The nurses asked them to keep it down, but they couldn't. When they called her name, and she and her dad went back to see the doctor, she explained that she wanted him to take her blood. She explained what happened earlier that day, and when the doctor got her results back, he asked her why she was wasting his time. Her dad hollered, and they walked out the hospital laughing. The joy of the Lord is my strength (Nehemiah 8:10)!

Mother Stacks told me about the time that she and Mother Boyd were in service at a church in Harrisburg, PA. and she died in the bathroom. She wasn't feeling well so Mother Boyd asked two of the sisters to take Mother Stacks to the bathroom. When Mother Stacks went inside the stall, she slid off the toilet to the floor and the sisters panicked. One of them ran upstairs to get Mother Boyd. When Mother Boyd got inside the bathroom, others were already inside and she put everyone out. She went inside the stall where Mother Stacks was and began calling her name as loud as she could. Mother Stacks said she felt like she was flying in the dark at a fast rate of speed but she could hear her name being called faintly.

She said, "The voice calling my name got louder and louder and I turned around and began flying back the opposite way." When her spirit came back in her body, her eyes opened and Mother Boyd was leaning over her. Mother Boyd told her to open her mouth and when she did, she blew in her mouth. She told her to open her mouth again and blew in her mouth again.

All of Mother Stacks' bodily fluids and waste were released from her when she died on the bathroom floor. Mother Boyd had her covered up in some throw cloths and her brother Cato took her to the hospital for the doctor to check her out. The doctor examined her and upon examining her clothes, he knew she had died. He gave her a clean bill of health. God is a miracle working God!

I remember one Sunday morning at Shalom when Mother Stacks got up to preach. When she got to the pulpit, the praise hit her feet, and she danced. All of a sudden, she ran through the church, laying hands as she went. People were hitting the floor left and right. When she got back to the pulpit, she ran to the back of the church, where a lady who had come to visit the church was. Mother Stacks "shot" her in her breast and came back in the pulpit.

The following Sunday night, the lady who had visited the prior Sunday came back. We were having testimony service, and the lady stood up to testify. She stated that she had gone to her doctor that week to have her mammogram. When the doctor looked at the mammogram, he told her, "This is not good. He informed her that she had breast cancer. She asked around to see if anyone knew where she could go and be healed, and someone told her to go up the street to the church on the corner of 14th and Poplar in Detroit, Michigan. She told me that when she got inside the building, "The Lady of God was praying for people, but she didn't pray for her." She said, "I asked God, please let the Lady of God come back and pray for me, and that's when Lady of God ran to the back and hit my breast." She fell back into the pew and stated she knew God had done it.

She went back to the doctor on Monday and asked him to do the mammogram over again. She said her doctor was hesitant, but she was persistent. She said when the doctor looked at the mammogram, he started scratching his head. He grabbed the mammogram from the week prior, which showed the cancer, and put it against the new one. He told her, "I don't know what happened, but you're cancer-free". We praised God for his healing power!

A lot of times, when Mother came to stay at my home, she would read the scriptures, and we would discuss them. She was happiest when God would reveal His word while we were studying His word. She would often say, "God, what do you mean, then she'd shake her head as if answering the Holy Spirit." She would look at me and answer the question she had just asked God, and it would go on for hours. Those were very precious moments that I'll never forget.

GOD TAKES CARE OF HIS CHILDREN

In 2014, my position with the partner I worked for at the law firm was taken from me and given to someone with more seniority because her boss was sick and would not return to work. I was assigned two first-year associates. Things were ok for a while, but one day, things went left. The Office Manager who worked there didn't like African Americans. One by one, she did everything in her power to get rid of the African Americans. She succeeded in many instances and set her sights on me.

Things went downhill fast. I was being harassed on a weekly basis. I would go in the bathroom stall and cry my eyes out because of the mistreatment. I asked God if I could quit, and He said, "No, I want you to sit here and go through all of it." I didn't know why I couldn't quit, but I knew I had to obey God, even when it was uncomfortable. During my lunch hour, I would call Mother Stacks or my friend Terrilyn, and all I would say when they answered the phone was, "Pray." God let me sit in that furnace of affliction for one year.

The company eventually got rid of the Office Manager, and in March 2015, they hired someone to take her place. One day, while working at my desk, they brought the new Office Manager to my desk to introduce him to me. When he got to my desk, I heard the Holy Spirit say, "The devil in him hates the God in you. He's going to be trouble." After greeting him, I continued working. A few weeks later, I was called into a meeting with the Secretarial Manager and the Office Manager. The Secretarial Manager was caught off guard. The Office Manager had written me up for something that I had not done. He asked me to sign the write-up, and I told him I wasn't signing anything that wasn't true. I walked out of the meeting, and he got angry.

I learned many things working in the legal industry. The Holy Spirit led me to get an attorney, and I did. I was told by my attorney to send an email to the Office Manager and his boss. I did as I was told, and based on my email, they knew I had consulted with legal counsel. I asked that I be able to see my personnel file and that they let me know when I could do so. Two days later, I was allowed to see my personnel file, and the Office Manager had taken everything out of it except one page. When I asked where all the documents were in my file, he lied and said they don't keep the correspondence in the employee files.

I looked him in the eye and said, "We both know that's not true." He turned red and said I had to sign the write-up. I told him I was not going to sign a lie. When I walked out the office, I said God, please get me out of here. The next morning, while in prayer, the Holy Spirit said, "Today they're going to terminate you, but they'll have to pay you to leave."

I was excited and asked God to let them have the meeting at 11:00 a.m. so I could take the 12:20 p.m. Metra train home. I went to work, and HR called me into the conference room at 11:00 a.m. The Office Manager said, "We know you have legal counsel, so we'd like to end your employment with a severance package. We'll give you half today, and we would like you and your attorney to read our documents regarding your lawsuit. If you sign our documents stating you won't sue us and get the documents back to us within six weeks, we'll mail you the second half of the severance."

I left the office at noon and was able to catch my 12:20 p.m. train. I blessed my God for victory in the midst of adversity. When I got home, I went inside my prayer closet. I said, "God, thank you for allowing me to get out of that toxic environment. I thank you for giving me patience while going through all the harassment I had to endure. Now God, I'm your responsibility, so I expect you to take care of me. Can I please have one year off work?"

When I came out of my prayer closet, I went to the bank and deposited my severance check. I came home and booked a flight to Orlando, Florida. Next, I called the Ritz-Carlton in Orlando, Florida, and booked a room for six nights. I booked spa treatments and treated myself royally while there. I bought a suitcase, went on a shopping spree, and filled up the suitcase I purchased.

When I got home from my trip, I went to the unemployment office and received unemployment for six months. The amount I received each month was not enough to pay my mortgage, nor any of my other bills. I would go into my prayer closet each morning and fellowship with the Lord, knowing that He would meeting every need.

It's something how in my first course of faith, I was begging God to open a door of employment during my season of lack. This time, I was asking for a year off, trusting that God would take care of me, and He did, supernaturally. I'm amazed by God on a day-to-day basis. I decided to go through with my lawsuit for discrimination. One night, my God-mother called me and said, "Rita, I was in prayer and the Lord told me to tell you not to sue. He's coming another way." I knew it was God because I had not told anyone about my plans to sue.

In December 2015, I was in my prayer closet talking to God and when I came out, I got my vacuum cleaner out of my linen closet and began vacuuming my bedroom floor. The Holy Spirit said, look in your nightstand drawer and get that Vanguard statement out. I said, "God, that's just a statement showing how much I'll have to pay in income taxes." The Holy Spirit repeated the same thing again so I turned off the vacuum cleaner and obeyed. When I looked inside the envelope, it was a letter from Vanguard addressed to me with a different account number. The Lord told me to call the number on the letter and ask the representative to explain what it was.

I did so and the representative put me on hold because she didn't know what it was. While I was on hold, the Holy Spirit said, "You remember when I told your Godmother to tell you don't sue, I'm coming another way?" I said, "Yes Lord." The Holy Spirit said, "I just came another way." God made the company pay me another lump sum of money and trust me, I didn't ask any questions.

My faith in God had grown over the years, so I knew God would take care of me. He came supernaturally every month and paid all my bills. There was no lack because God supplied all my needs. I'm eternally grateful for all God does on my behalf.

WHEN WE BELIEVE, WE RECEIVE

At the time of my annual Retreat February 2016, I had been off work for eleven months. At the end of the Retreat, I said to the attendees, "God is opening a door of employment for me, and I'm going to come back and testify about it." Wednesday night, following my Retreat, the Holy Spirit said, "Pull up Executive Legal Assistant jobs on your cell phone." When I did so, I saw a job listing for a law firm in downtown Chicago. I responded via email and attached my resume from my cell phone.

That Friday morning, I received an email from the company asking if I could come in for an interview. I responded and had an interview on Monday at 9:00 a.m. I met with two partners: one in Corporate Law and one in Trust and Estates. The interview went well, and a week later, I was offered the position. I went back to the company to discuss salary, among other things, about the position.

That Monday morning, I went downtown and met with HR, and they offered me a salary of $50,000. I politely declined the offer and asked the HR Director to thank both partners for meeting with me. I turned to get my coat off the back of the chair I was sitting in, and he asked, "What's the least amount you would accept?" I turned my face to the wall like

Hezekiah and inquired of God. The Holy Spirit said, "Tell him $62,000 a year." I was like what? To me, it wasn't enough, but I knew I had to obey God.

I told the HR Director, and when he left the conference room, the Holy Spirit started singing the song, "You're a Good Good Father." I began rocking in my seat to the song, and the HR Director came back with positive news. I started the job the following Monday, but God wasn't finished yet.

In April 2017, I was in service with Mother Stacks, and she came to me and said, "There's another job coming. You're going to travel like you did at first, and God's going to bless you." I received the word of the Lord and began putting it into action. I taught a message on 1st Timothy 1:18-19 which says, "This charge I commit unto thee, son Timothy, according to the prophecies which went before on thee, that thou by them mightiest war a good warfare; Holding faith, and a good conscience. . ."

The Lord taught me you don't watch prophecies; you war prophecies in. A few months later, an attorney whom I worked for at a previous law firm texted me regarding an employment opportunity. She asked if she could call me that evening and explain the position to me. I agreed, and we discussed the position during the call. A week later, I worked half a day and traveled to Lisle, Illinois to meet with three of the executives at the company.

After the interview, the HR Director came in and asked that I complete the job application and take a drug test. I did so, and as of the writing of this book, God did exactly what He promised. I travel like I did when I got my first job at a law firm, and God has blessed me and continues to do so while working for the company.

OBEYING GOD CONCERNING MINISTRY

God's hand has been on my life for many years. I accepted my call to the ministry at the age of 24. God would raise me up, and the leaders I was under would sit me down. I remained faithful to God's call on my life even when it was difficult to do so. In September 2011, the Holy Spirit said, "I want you to get your EIN number for your ministry." I asked God, " What's the name of my ministry?" He replied, "Lord & Elegance Ministries." He said, " As long as you keep me first, I'll lead, guide, and direct you."

God gave me favor with a paralegal at the law firm I was working for at the time. She filled out the necessary paperwork, and I received my EIN number for my ministry a few weeks later. The Lord spoke to me and said, I want you to have a Women's Retreat, and I want the theme to be, "Come Away My Beloved." When God spoke those words to me, I hesitated because I knew there would be problems with those who were in authority in ministry.

One Saturday morning, I got up at 5:30 a.m. and talked to God. I laid back down and went straight into a dream. In the dream, I was in a service with Mother Boyd. At the end of the service, I took her home and helped her into the house. I cooked her something to eat, and she and I sat down at the table. She looked at me and said, "Daughter, I shot you with a work to do for God. If you don't finish the work, you can't come up here where I am." I came out of the dream saying, "Yes, Lord."

I made plans for my first Retreat. I created my flyers and negotiated prices for hotel rooms and meals. The Holy Spirit taught me how to create my website, and after everything was solidified, I sent out my flyers. My Godmother came to town, and I showed her my website. She asked why I was having a Retreat, and I told her because God told me to do so. Your obedience to God must be your number one priority when it comes to doing exactly what He said. I decided right then and there that if I had to walk it out by myself, I would do so.

Prior to my Retreat, I had not been in contact with my god sister Rita Ball for some years. One day, the Lord told me to invite her to my Retreat. I said God, I don't know how to get in touch with Rita. He said, "She works at The Pointe at Kilpatrick in Crestwood, Illinois. Call and ask to speak to her." I obeyed, and when Rita answered the phone, I asked her how she was doing. She was very guarded on the call, but I did what the Holy Spirit led me to do. She registered for the Retreat and came.

I had my first Retreat the weekend of March 17, 2012. The Lord had me to reach out to my friends Terrilyn Franklin and Yvonne Oby to be speakers along with myself at the Saturday morning service. Terrilyn spoke on the Prayer of Petition. I spoke on the Prayer of Forgiveness. Yvonne Oby's subject was the Prayer of Deliverance. That evening, the Lord had me to teach on the foundations of Holiness; not an outward display but an inner transformation. Yeah God!

After I concluded my message, Rita Ball was the first person the Lord had me to call up. He prayed for her and spoke into her life. She was in a backslidden state, and God reclaimed her soul back to Himself. The next morning, the Lord told me to have the women to speak about what God did for them. Rita was the first one to come up. She testified about how God reclaimed her and healed her at the same time.

She shared how she was dealing with a tumor in her breast and stated that when she showered that morning, the tumor was gone. God is a rewarder of obedience. Many other women spoke about God's miraculous power and what the Retreat did for them. When all odds were stacked against me, God put his approval on Lord & Elegance Ministries, and I'm eternally grateful for all God continues to do on our behalf.

In 2013, we had our second retreat, and God's presence was there to heal and deliver. I prayed for many people that Saturday night. God had me to call a woman up to pray for her, and when she came up to the front, the Lord took my hand and went from her neck down her spine and said, "If you don't let this go, it's going to take you out of here." The lady screamed, and I hugged her. She and I went down to the floor, and I laid her on her side. As I prayed for her, she began to purge. God set her free that night.

When I got to my hotel room, I got on my face and asked God, " Were you pleased with the service tonight?" The Lord spoke to me and said, "I'm going to place an honor on you that no man can take." I sat up and meditated on the words He spoke to me. Monday, while on my lunch hour at work, I received a phone call from Dr. Sandra Robinson of Kingdom of Heaven University. She told me I came highly recommended for a doctorate program and wanted me to be part of it. I said to her, "I'm not interested, but thank you so much for calling."

When I hung up the phone, the Lord said, "That's Me, now call her back and repent." I said, "God, I'm so sorry." I called her back and repented, and she asked if she could call me back at the same time tomorrow. I agreed and got off the phone.

Tuesday, while working, the Lord said, "Get up and go to lunch and sit on the side of the building where no one comes." As soon as I sat down, Dr. Robinson called. She said, "I talked to God about you last night, and He said some things to me about you." She told me all about my life from the time I was a child, all the way up to my Retreat two days prior. I was crying so hard because I knew no one could have spoken to her but God. She said, "You will be part of this doctorate program, and all I need from you is the fee for your robe, collar, cap, and degree." She hung up, and I spent the next 20 minutes getting myself together to go back and finish out my day at work.

In April 2013, God gave me my Doctor of Divinity degree from Kingdom of Heaven University. The enemy fought me with a feeling of intimidation because once God gave it to me, word got out, and church folk weren't happy about it. God said I did this for you because of your faithfulness to me. You will not allow the enemy to talk you out of what I've given you. I said, "Yes, Lord."

While in prayer one night, the Lord spoke to me and said I want you to have an all-night shut-in at the Hilton Suites Hotel in Oak Brook, Illinois. He said, "Title it, 'One Night With Christ.'" Then He told me to anoint some oil according to Exodus 30:22-25. I obeyed and put the oil in a big glass half-gallon jar and put it in my prayer closet. I called the hotel under the unction of the Holy Spirit and spoke to the sales and catering manager. When I told her what I wanted to do, she said the hotel could not accommodate my request. I was informed that the hotel doesn't rent out its event rooms overnight. I asked to speak to a manager, and she said he would tell me the same thing. I know that wherever God guides, He provides, so I was persistent in speaking with the manager of the hotel. The next day, the sales and catering manager called back and said I can't believe this, but the manager agreed to let you have your overnight event. I wasn't surprised.

The Lord had me to buy some small amber glass bottles and fill each one with the blessed oil. He asked me to type up the significance of the anointing oil and give it along with the oil to each delegate. He also told me to go out and buy white comforters and buy some red ribbon to tie a bow around each comforter for each delegate. I did so, and Rita and I packed everything into my SUV.

That Friday night at 8:00 p.m., I spoke about repentance, transparency, unforgiveness, and moving on. After my message, the Lord had each lady to come up to get their oil and comforter. At 9:00 p.m., the women were told to find a place in the room and wrap up in their comforters.

Pastor Terrilyn and I prayed for hours and hours. The Lord prompted me to walk around the room and pray for individual women that the enemy was antagonizing, and they were set free. We stopped prayer at 5:00 a.m. and allowed the women to have an hour of quiet time.

Saturday evening, we came back for a spirit-filled service and Pastor Terrilyn preached with signs following. Sunday morning, the Lord had me to allow the women to tell what God did for them. There was a woman who came Friday night, and when I put oil on her head, the spirit of the Lord told her, "No one has a right to abuse you." I hugged her and shared how much Jesus loves her, and she wept bitterly. Sunday, when she came up, she stated that her husband had been abusing her for years. She wanted to stay after the shut in was over but didn't have the money. She walked around the event room like Joshua walked around the walls of Jericho. She said, "God, I don't have any money, but I need to be here until it's over."

At that time, the young lady who had invited her decided to go back in the event room and saw her walking around the walls. She ended up paying for her room on Saturday morning, and the young lady was able to stay. She said, "When I got up to my room, I took a shower and with nothing but the suit God gave me, I wrapped up in that comforter and asked God to finish what He started. God loved on me like I had never been loved on before, and He gave me my confidence back. I now realize that no one has a right to abuse me because Jesus loves me". There wasn't a dry eye in the room. I'm always amazed at the depth of the love of Jesus and how He shows His people how much He loves them.

One year, the Lord had me to have a "Breakthrough in Praise" Retreat. The grandson of the Pastor's church that I grew up in fell on my heart. God asked me to call him and invite him to play for our services. I didn't understand because we already had a musician, but I obeyed the voice of God.

I called Eric and explained to him what I needed from him, and he obliged. We were having a Saturday morning, Saturday night, and Sunday morning service. My Godmother Dr. Stacks was in town to be in attendance, so we traveled to the Hilton Hotel Saturday morning for the Retreat. When I got to the hotel and went in the event room, I saw Eric and my musician hooking up the keyboard and amplifier. When I saw the state Eric was in, I immediately started crying. I couldn't stop. I went from crying to travailing in the spirit.

Mother Stacks whispered, "You've got to get yourself together because it's time to get started." I asked Pastor Terrilyn to open up the service with prayer because I couldn't stop crying. Once the service ended, a light buffet breakfast was served, and I told Eric to go and get food. Everyone left to go into their hotel rooms. When I walked out of the room, I asked Eric if he was waiting for his ride. He said he was just going to sit there in the hallway until the evening service. I asked him to give me a few minutes.

I called my musician Antoinne and asked him to let Eric stay in his room until I called him back. I called Rita (our treasurer) and told her we needed to get Eric a hotel room, and she made it happen. Rita had given me an envelope with $126 in it from people who would not be able to attend the entire weekend and wanted to bless me. Eric had lost his mother to breast cancer at a young age and was trying to survive the best way he could.

When I got to my room, I decided I was going to go the Carson Pirie Scott to buy Eric some necessities. I texted him and asked for all his sizes. My Godmother knocked on my door and asked was I going to get the young man some things, and I said yes. She grabbed her purse and we went to the mall. I had a lot of things that rang up to about $1,200 but many of them were on sale. I had 20% off coupons and asked God for favor. I bought Eric shirts, sweaters, khaki pants, and everything else that a young man needed, and my Godmother bought him dress shirts, dress pants, and a suit jacket.

What should have cost me $600 cost me $126! What should have cost my Godmother $1,600 cost her $600 because of the coupons. When I got back to my hotel room, I called Antoinne down to my room. I asked him to check Eric into his hotel room, take the clothes me and my Godmother bought, run him a bath, cut his hair, and give him the toiletries so that he could get himself ready for the evening service. Antoinne had tears running down his face. He said, "Dr. Rita, this is what ministry looks like." I hugged him and told him how much I appreciated him.

That evening, when my Godmother and I walked into the room, Eric was dressed in the suit, and when I looked at him, he smiled at me and gave me a thumbs up. After I taught, the Lord had me to pray for different people. When I called Eric up, the Lord had me to have Dr. Stacks pray for him. She put oil on his head and his hands and asked, "Young man, what do you want?" Eric replied, "I want to live."

I bent over in travail, and so did Terrilyn. We wept for that young man until his breakthrough came. Thank you, Jesus! Everyone ate dinner after the service was over, so I told Eric to get food. Sunday morning, when the service ended, I went to Eric and gave him some money for coming to play the keyboard. He said, "Dr. Rita, no one has ever done anything like this for me since my mother died." Tears welled up in my eyes, and I hugged him. I said, "Eric, please keep in touch with me and let me know if you need anything."

Eric began calling me after the Retreat. He said, "Dr. Rita, I have never witnessed the power of God like that before in my life. Can I please just come and be a part of your services?" I said, "Absolutely." Whenever I had services and had my Godmother in services, I would invite Eric, and he would come. One night when we were talking on the phone, the

Lord told me to tell Eric he had to forgive his family members who hurt him.

I explained to Eric what forgiveness was, and he listened intently. I said, "Eric, you will know when you have forgiven because when you reach back to that place of hurt, it won't be there." We would talk every other week, and one night Eric called me. He was so excited. I asked him what happened, and he explained that relationships with family members that he had not spoken to in years were restored! I was so happy for him. Unfortunately, Eric passed away a few years later. God gave me an audience with Eric when it mattered. I'm so grateful for all God does, and I'm amazed by the excellent ways he does them. He doeth all things well! Mark 7:37

Lord & Elegance Ministries continues to host annual conferences and luncheons each year in Illinois. We have also hosted retreats outside of Illinois as well, like the "Restored in the Wilderness" Retreat in Petoskey, Michigan inside of a beautiful cabin, and God restored everyone in attendance. We had a "Command Your Mountain" Retreat in Orlando, Florida, and spoke about the power in our words. We had a "He Always Causes Me to Triumph" Retreat in Las Vegas at the Venetian Hotel and spoke about the Fight is Fixed; We Win.

I am always amazed at God's miraculous power. I pray that you have been encouraged and your faith has been strengthened while reading this book. Always remember, there is nothing too hard for God.

ABOUT THE AUTHOR

Dr. Rita is known for being an encourager to the body of Christ. She has had many encounters with God, and God has consistently demonstrated His power in her life. She is one of God's Prophets and is a Teacher of the gospel of our Lord Jesus Christ.

God has entrusted Dr. Rita with Lord & Elegance Ministries, which is a ministry of love, healing, and restoration. She operates in the word of wisdom, word of knowledge, faith, gifts of healing, and discerning of spirits. She loves the Lord and His people. Her heart's desire is to see the people of God free to be who He has called them to be for His glory.

Learn more about
upcoming events with
Dr. Rita Newell

Scan or call:
(630) 777-8176

Dr. Rita Newell hosts annual and special events
throughout the year to encourage women, men, and
their families to live for God. If you are looking to
have a divine appointment with God to renew your
body, heart, mind, faith, commitment, or to connect
and give your life to God, join her at her next event
and encounter her heart ministry to serve the people
of God.

LORD & ELEGANCE
MINISTRIES

LordAndEleganceMinistries.com

SCAN ME

Call or Text:
770-240-0089 Press Extension 1
Web: KLEpub.com
Email Services@klepub.com

It's time to start and finish **YOUR Story**!

KLE Publishing specializes in helping people become authors. In as little as 15 to 90 days, we can help you develop your books and e-books and publish to 39,000 outlets! We also offer audiobook services.

Write, Edit, Format, Publish
We can help from
Start to Finish.

Explore and learn more about published authors affiliated with KLE.

KLEPub.com